# SALINAS
# PUEBLO
# MISSIONS

= ABÓ = QUARAI = GRAN QUIVIRA =

# SALINAS PUEBLO MISSIONS

= NATIONAL MONUMENT, NEW MEXICO =

## Dan Murphy

(left) *Petroglyphs near Abó.*

WESTERN NATIONAL PARKS ASSOCIATION

# Estancia Basin

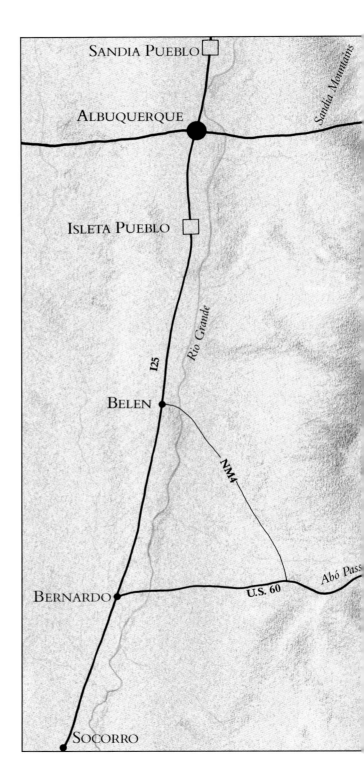

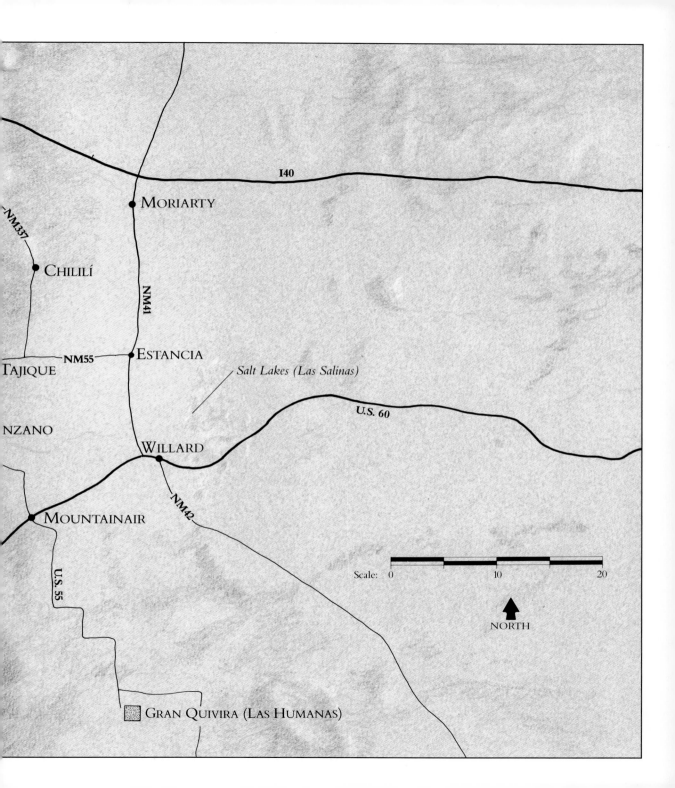

I40

● MORIARTY

NM337

● CHILILÍ

NM41

NM55

● ESTANCIA

*Salt Lakes (Las Salinas)*

TAJIQUE

NZANO

U.S. 60

WILLARD ●

NM42

● MOUNTAINAIR

U.S. 55

Scale: 0      10      20

NORTH

▓ GRAN QUIVIRA (LAS HUMANAS)

Section One

# BEGINNINGS

(above) *Salinas red olla from Pueblo de Las Humanas at Gran Quivira.*

(left) *Mission of San Buenaventura ruins, Gran Quivira.*

*Carved schist buffalo effigy from Las Humanas.*

In the middle of New Mexico, the grama-grass plains of the Estancia Basin spread like a tan carpet between desert mountain ranges. A lone bee patrols the purple cholla cactus blossoms, and the red and yellow "firewheels" turn slowly to follow the sun. Broad pastures, with fences that disappear in the distance, rise to the gentle highlands surrounding this basin.

Here in this remote, quiet valley, the weathered ruins of three Indian villages and their Spanish colonial missions are preserved in the three units of Salinas Pueblo Missions National Monument. The silence belies the remarkable human history of this place, and the ultimately tragic drama that unfolded here in the seventeenth century, when the expanding empire of Spain finally reached these peaceful Indian towns.

The bedrock that rims this basin lies almost hidden beneath the dark green pinyon and juniper trees. Part of it is the dark red shale and sandstone of the Abó formation, laid down on coastal plains 250 million years ago. To the south the outcrops are gray, slightly younger San Andres limestone, formed when Permian seas swept over southern New Mexico. To the west rise the dramatically upswept blocks of the Sandia and Manzano mountain ranges, and to the east are the low, hard granite Pedernals.

Even to the casual observer, the Estancia Basin looks as though it could have been a lake, and it once was. Just ten thousand

1

years ago, recent as geologists count time, glaciers covered much of North America. Though the great ice sheets did not come as far south as New Mexico, temperatures here were slightly cooler then. More rain and snow fell than the sun could evaporate, and the basin filled with water.

Aerial photographs reveal concentric "bathtub rings" of beach line where the ancient lake paused as it rose or fell. Water ran into this basin, but usually did not have a way out. Runoff from the surrounding area washed minerals into the lake and, as water evaporated, these minerals were left behind and concentrated. Fossils of *Protelphidium obiculare*, a tiny salt water "foram," have been found in the Estancia Basin bedrock, which confirms that the ancient lake was brackish.

People first saw the sun sparkling on that lake millennia ago. They camped by lake-feeding streams and by springs, occasionally leaving behind tools and other artifacts. Today they are called the Clovis people, named for the New Mexico town where their artifacts were first found.

Ten thousand years ago Clovis families looked out on a different Estancia Basin than we see today. The area was green then, not red-brown desert. Rain brought its blessing to grass and moss, to bushes and trees. Elephant-like mammoths lumbered across the grasslands. Clovis people scavenged the great animals but occasionally hunted them, too—no small feat for people who only had stone weapons. Camels, giant sloth, and *Bison antiquus*, the huge, now-extinct relative of today's bison—all were familiar to Clovis people who ranged the country.

As the mammoths disappeared, hunters relied more on bison. With different needs they developed different tools, enough so that anthropologists give these later people a new name, the Folsom Culture. The Folsom lance point is a masterpiece of flint-knapping, difficult to reproduce even today.

Evidence of these early Clovis and Folsom cultures is scant. They left little, save a few camp or kill sites and some marvelously made Folsom points. Yet it is evidence enough to know people lived here, in a world greatly different from our own. Imagine the taste of prehistoric mammoth and bison, and what it must have been like to face them with only stone-tipped weapons.

Over centuries the climate warmed, and the great ice sheets to the north retreated. Precipitation decreased while evaporation increased. With the drying came the dying, and the great herds slowly became extinct. Lake Estancia also disappeared, leaving behind a brown-green grassy bowl with low-lying "salines" that become ephemeral salt ponds during the short rainy season.

The small bands of people living off the land adapted. In their constant search for food, these people rarely stayed in one place for long. They hunted small game when it was available, and gathered ripe pinyon nuts in the mountains and fat yucca pods in the flats. The land was a giant pantry to them.

*Now-extinct relatives of bison were once hunted by prehistoric Clovis people in the Estancia Basin.*

3

*Ruins of Pueblo de Las Humanas, Gran Quivira.*

*Section Two*

# SETTLING DOWN

Somewhere in central Mexico, whether accidentally or deliberately, prehistoric people discovered how to cultivate and breed certain wild grasses to produce a plant with large, nutritious seeds. The resulting plant also held its seeds, instead of scattering them as most wild plants do. Today we call that human-produced plant corn, and it touched off an agricultural revolution in the Americas.

As revolutions go, it was a slow one. It took thousands of years, but the final results are plain in the record of the Estancia Basin. The culture of small, widely scattered hunter-gatherer bands eventually was transformed into the settled society of town-dwellers the Spaniards met. Corn was the catalyst for this fundamental change.

With the introduction of corn, people began to settle down. Corn was a reliable source of food that could be grown deliberately, and stored. But it had its price. Corn had to be planted because, unlike wild plants, it did not "volunteer" well. It behooved people to water the corn and protect it from birds and rodents.

Wandering bands began to leave members behind to tend these special plants, and later beans and squash, while the main parties walked on to find familiar wild food plants ripening somewhere else. The ones who stayed behind had to improvise shelter, instead of simply camping under the nearest bower or rock overhang. Deep in the archeological record of the Estancia Basin, about A.D. 600, pithouses appear.

The settling down of the people around the Estancia Basin was part of a very large trend in the desert Southwest. Traces of prehistoric pithouses are found throughout what is now northern New Mexico and Arizona, and southern Colorado and Utah. For a thousand years they were the principal type of dwelling.

Designs were not rigid. Pithouses could be shallow or quite deep. Usually they were round, but some were rectangular with rounded corners, and a few were just square. The superstructure could be as simple as brush stuck into the ground around the hole and tied over to make a dome. It might be made of interwoven branches covered with clay.

Some pithouses were almost permanent, with a framework of posts and timbers to support the roof. Some were entered through a doorway, often through an antechamber, which gave the pithouse a figure-eight plan. Those with a firmer superstructure were entered through a hatchway in the roof, using a ladder. A hearth near the center of the floor supplied light and heat, and hollows dug into the floor provided storage.

Early pithouses were widely scattered, but later they were built in clusters to form pithouse villages. Eventually, regional architectural styles developed.

At about the same time that pithouse villages were emerging in the Estancia Basin, the area's language pattern probably was set. People who spoke Tiwa, and who lived in the Rio Grande Valley near today's Albuquerque, apparently migrated in increasing numbers through the pass in Tijeras Canyon and occupied the northern part of the basin. Piro-speaking people living further south in the Rio Grande Valley, in the vicinity of Socorro, worked their way through Abó Pass and settled at the lower edge of the basin.

Five or six centuries after the time of Christ, people in the Estancia Basin began to produce pottery. Nomadic people did not develop pottery. It was too heavy and fragile to travel. But for people who settled in one place, pottery made it possible to develop new cooking techniques, collect water, and provide rodent-proof storage.

As with architecture, distinctive regional pottery styles also emerged. By studying the characteristics of pottery fragments, archeologists have been able to document how the interaction between the people of the Estancia Basin and distant villages changed over time.

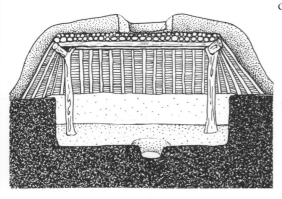

*People of the Estancia Basin first began to build permanent pithouses about A.D. 600.*

One Estancia Basin archeological survey counted pieces of broken pottery at sites from the time of the pithouses, and found about sixty-six percent were brownwares, indicating either influence or actual trade from the south. This evidence suggests that the people who first established permanent settlements in the Estancia Basin were influenced by the Mogollon (MUGGY-own) culture.

At sites occupied two centuries later, only seventeen percent of the potsherds found were brownwares, while the rest showed a definite shift to influence from a more advanced civilization centered on the Colorado Plateau to the north and west: the Anasazi.

Anasazi is a Navajo word that means, variously, "ancient people who are not us," "ancient ancestors" or "enemy of the old ones," depending on how the word is pronounced. The nomadic Navajo migrated onto the northwest Colorado Plateau shortly after prehistoric people had abandoned the area. The newcomers found spectacular village ruins in an empty land, and archeologists later used the Navajo term to refer to the prehistoric ancestors of all Puebloan people.

Change did not happen simultaneously throughout the Anasazi world. It would emerge in one area, then stall, go slowly somewhere else; or it could spread quickly. One example is the use of the "jacal" (hah-CALL) structure, a wicker wall of woven sticks filled and coated thoroughly with mud. Near the end of the "jacal period," Anasazi builders developed a hybrid masonry style, in which jacal walls were built on stone foundations and faced with stone slabs. An excellent example of this is visible at the Abó Ruins of Salinas Pueblo Mission National Monument.

The emergence of jacal construction was part of a larger change that occurred throughout the Anasazi world: the movement to above-ground living. Anasazi stone structures began to appear about A.D. 900. Apparently they were used for storage at first, but eventually people moved into them.

The transition to above-ground living was not instantaneous, nor even rapid. Likely there were seasonal changes. One easily imagines living in warmer pithouses in the winter and moving to airier jacals or even stone houses in the hot summer. Even after masonry architecture had achieved astonishing sophistication in the twelfth century, some people still chose to live alongside in ancient pithouses year round.

The Estancia Basin was hardly the center of Anasazi culture, and change evidently came more slowly out on the edge of Anasazi civilization. Through trade and travel, the people of the Estancia Basin must have learned about the astonishing accomplishments of their cultural cousins in Chaco Canyon, two hundred miles northwest. But while architecture, trade, art, and ceremonialism reached their apogee at Chaco during the tenth century, the Estancia Basin people still lived in pithouses exclusively.

The Mesa Verde area bloomed shortly after A.D. 1150, and new pottery, tremendous buildings, and greater ceremonialism emerged from the cultural ferment. But not until about 1300, when Mesa Verde was abandoned, did stone towns begin to rise in the Estancia Basin.

*Section Three*

# TOWNS ON THE LANDSCAPE

Movement of peoples is not easy to trace. It is rather like the shallow water running along the sandy bed of the Rio Grande in August—the geologists' "braided stream." A broad stream may split into two or more smaller rivulets, with braids that may or may not rejoin. Occasionally one of these smaller strands curls off by itself, becomes isolated, and dies in the sun.

When Mesa Verde was abandoned about 1300 the departing Anasazi did not pack up as a group and march down to the Rio Grande Valley. Yet over time the Indian villages there, along with Zuni, Acoma, and Hopi towns farther west, became the new centers of Anasazi culture. While the population in the Rio Grande Valley burgeoned during the fourteenth century, the Estancia Basin, easily accessible through the Tijeras and Abó mountain passes, also experienced rapid growth.

Several stone villages and towns developed in the Estancia Basin during this period. The ruins of three are preserved at Salinas Pueblo Missions National Monument: Quarai or "Cuarac," Abó, and Gran Quivira, or "Las Humanas" as it would be named by the first Spaniards to arrive in the area. These three form a triangle, with Quarai and Abó about ten miles apart on the northwest side of the basin, and Las Humanas about thirty miles southeast.

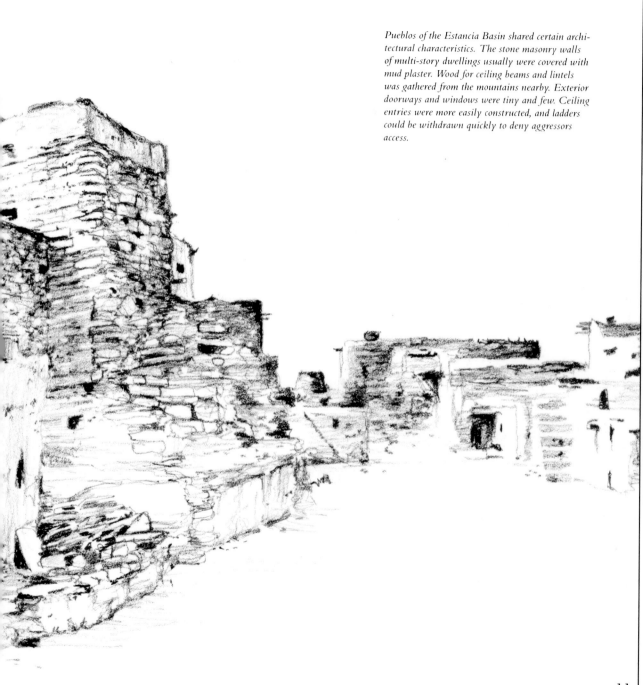

Pueblos of the Estancia Basin shared certain architectural characteristics. The stone masonry walls of multi-story dwellings usually were covered with mud plaster. Wood for ceiling beams and lintels was gathered from the mountains nearby. Exterior doorways and windows were tiny and few. Ceiling entries were more easily constructed, and ladders could be withdrawn quickly to deny aggressors access.

11

## QUARAI

Quarai is set in a juniper forest that slopes toward a tree-lined, spring-fed stream, which flows from the base of the Manzano Mountains. This stream trickles eastward through land the people farmed, to the salines out in the Estancia Basin. Timber and game abound in the nearby mountains, and plentiful red sandstone makes a fine building material.

Quarai residents spoke Tiwa. Early archeological testing hinted that Quarai was built, then abandoned, and later reoccupied. Later surveys found material dating from the supposed missing period, which tends to disprove the abandonment idea. Visitors might agree that Quarai was just too beautiful, and the living too easy, for anyone to leave, unless extraordinary circumstances compelled them to do so.

## ABÓ

Abó was built on another outcrop of the same red sandstone, around the shoulder of the Manzano Mountains from Quarai and astride the trail to Abó Pass, which leads to the Rio Grande Valley. Abó, too, stood beside a cluster of springs giving rise to a precious desert stream. The mountains are farther away from Abó than from Quarai, but Abó had the advantage of being on the trade route through the pass. Despite their relative proximity to Quarai, the people of Abó spoke Tompiro.

## LAS HUMANAS

On rocky, gray Chupadero Mesa, which forms the south edge of the Estancia Basin, stand remnants of the round stone house that was the beginning of Las Humanas. As with Quarai and Abó, Las Humanas was built from the rock upon which it stood. The building became an impressive structure of perhaps 240 rooms arranged in concentric circles around a central kiva.

The Tompiro-speaking community of Las Humanas had trade advantages as the settlement nearest the nomadic Indians who lived on the plains to the south and east. Also, the sandy soil nearby was good for raising corn. Still, water was more scarce at Las Humanas than at Quarai and Abó, which had streams nearby. The people at

*Alibates flint for this large knife from Las Humanas was quarried in northwest Texas.*

*Razor-sharp Chalcedony (translucent quartz) point with equally-spaced side notches, from Las Humanas.*

Las Humanas compensated as best they could, building surface water catchment systems, cisterns, and wells.

It is easy to see what the Indians of the Estancia Basin built; the ruins are in the park. They made houses from stone gathered locally and wood from the mountains nearby. These buildings were not at all like modern farmers' houses. Rooms were small because available timbers used to support the roofs usually were short. Small rooms also were easier to heat.

Doorways were tiny and few, in part because doors were difficult to make and operate without metal tools and hinges, which were unknown to American Indians. Moreover, an exterior doorway, even if closed, was a weak spot that was difficult to defend. Ceiling hatchways were easier to make and protect. Ladders were used to climb up to the roof and then down through the hatch. In the event of an attack, defenders could deny the aggressors access by simply withdrawing the ladders.

Rooms were sparsely furnished and served principally as a refuge from bad weather or enemies. Judging from where the tools and "stuff of life" they left behind have been found, it is evident the people slept, cooked, and worked outside most of the time.

Anasazi town planning always included a plaza. In fact, much more everyday life went on in the plaza than in the rooms. Women made pottery and cooked, kids harassed barking dogs, turkeys looked for loose grain, and men chipped projectile points from imported stone. There were fires for warmth, for cooking, and for firing pottery. Virtually every stick of wood for miles around a town was scavenged.

After making the transition from below-ground to above-ground living, the people did not totally forget those pithouses. Instead, the form became the *kiva*, the underground ceremonial chamber that occured throughout the Anasazi world. In many ways life in the Estancia Basin Indian towns centered around the kivas. Kivas were entered through a hatch in the roof, which also served as a chimney for the firepit. Sometimes the walls were painted with elaborate designs, such as those found at Las Humanas.

Descendants of those people still use kivas today, and choose to keep much of their religious life private. Still, judging from the effort that went into ancient kiva construction, the ceremonial year must have been as rich then as now. Dances with steps and stories passed down since ancient times are still performed throughout the year, to keep the universe in order, reverse the change in day's length, or bring rains.

Occasionally, trusted visitors may be permitted to hear the stories of these people, their gods, and their wanderings. These stories were once told around the stone homes and in the kivas of Quarai, Abó, and Las Humanas. Life moved around and through kivas in a way modern visitors might not recognize.

The people made no clear distinction between the secular and the sacred. Planting corn and beans was as much a religious act as praying for rain to help them grow. Life depended on both. There was a ceremony for everything: hunting, planting, harvesting, rejoicing and mourning, marriage, and death.

The people were dryland farmers, but this was chancy land for agriculture. Water was a problem, and so was the short growing season. If the people escaped the danger of a late frost and the equal danger of an early one, and if the rains came, then the harvest could be bountiful. Several varieties of corn, squash, beans, and cotton were grown around the Estancia Basin. Amaranth seed was used, and likely was cultivated rather than simply gathered. Corn was a staple, of course, and it took much of a village's effort to plant, protect, and water. But even with seed strains and techniques adapted to this dry climate more than 6,000 feet above sea level, some years the crops faired poorly. Archeological evidence reveals that the people suffered the effects of occasional malnutrition.

The Anasazi were hunters as well as farmers. Rabbits, pronghorn, turkey, deer, even the mighty bison ended up in their stewpots. The people of the Estancia Basin hunted more than their Anasazi cousins elsewhere. One of the surprises found by archeological excavation at Las Humanas was the unexpectedly high ratio of animal bones to potsherds in the trash: about seventy bones per hundred sherds. At Badger House ruin in Mesa Verde National Park the ratio was less than two bones for every hundred sherds. The people also continued to gather wild seeds and plants—archeologists have found many pinyon shells on floors and around doorways.

*Golden eagle bone flute.*

In modern Pueblo Indian villages, most dwellings are occupied at any given time. A few rooms, and sometimes a whole cluster, may be abandoned, while new rooms are added. Old villages, too, were modified constantly. Sometimes whole sections were abandoned, while new construction happened on the "other side of town." In other cases, new structures were built directly over ruins of the old.

Archeologist Alden Hayes, during a dig in the 1960s, found something like that at Las Humanas. Sifting though the ruins, he discovered that about A.D. 1550 a new, semi-rectangular houseblock was constructed atop the ruins of the original circular house. The older structure, built 250 years earlier, had been abandoned, although the

*Pueblo people often built new dwellings directly over abandoned room blocks. Excavation revealed three layers of construction at Las Humanas. The site plan shows how the early-phase fourteenth-century circular structure lies beneath the late-phase, sixteenth-century rectangular building.*

kiva at its center had been maintained and a retaining wall had been built to keep crumbling debris from collapsing into the kiva. Apparently a good part of the new building was planned and built all at once, because a long wall with no obvious joints connects many units.

The rebuilding coincided with the introduction of a new kind of pottery, Tabirá Black-on-white, which replaced the Chupadero Black-on-white style that had been favored by Las Humanas residents for many generations. Sherds of the new pottery were found on the floors of the new rooms.

Also about A.D. 1550 the people at Las Humanas began to cremate their dead, after centuries of burials. A change this profound must have been preceded by some very serious discussion in the kivas.

The introduction of rectangular building plans, the Tabirá pottery style, and the practice of cremation may well have arrived with a group of immigrants from the Zuni-Cibola area, two hundred miles west through Abó Pass. Did something happen to compel these people to risk a permanent move to the Estancia Basin?

On July 7, 1540, gunfire exploded the silence of the southwestern desert for the first time. Vásquez de Coronado, a young explorer extending the northern fringes of the Spanish Empire in the New World, had arrived at the Zuni Pueblo of Hawikuh. After brief consideration, Coronado accepted the counsel of his priests, and ordered his troops to attack. That violent encounter in the Zuni area may well have precipitated the large-scale emigration to Las Humanas. The gunfire must have echoed in the Estancia Basin as the story tumbled from the lips of the newcomers. Strange and powerful men from across the sea had arrived.

*Red Kotyití Glaze-polychrome olla from Las Humanas.*

*Chupadero Black-on-white olla from Las Humanas.*

*Tabirá Black-on-white canteen from Las Humanas.*

*Tabirá Polychrome with stylized feathers from Las Humanas.*

*Section Four*

# MEN FROM ACROSS THE SEA

The astonishing arrival of helmeted, mounted Europeans in New Mexico would change the Estancia Basin forever. But the New Mexico experience was only an ember blown from a bonfire raging almost worldwide. By the late fifteenth century European sailing and navigational technology had carried explorers and merchants in expanding waves throughout the known world. In 1492, the famous voyage of Christopher Columbus suddenly added two new continents to that world. Then began an era of exploration like nothing seen before or since.

Ships of Spain, France, Britain, Portugal, and the Netherlands explored new coastlines, seeking commerce or conquest. Often it was difficult to distinguish between the two. The vagaries of wind and wave brought the Spaniards first to the islands of the Caribbean, then to Central and South America. Once New Spain was well-established in Mexico, exploration parties were sent in all directions.

The era of exploration reached something of a climax in the 1540s. At the time Coronado arrived at Hawikuh, an event that may have caused emigrants to flee to towns in the Estancia Basin, Spain had numerous other expeditions underway. Hernando de Soto was slogging through Florida and much of the Southeast, while Juan Rodríguez Cabrillo was pushing his tiny fleet up the California coast. Other Spanish expeditions were establishing the route to the Philippines, and continuing exploration of South America.

21

Coronado's journey north from New Spain to New Mexico was long, difficult, and dangerous. Unlike the *conquistadores* of Central and South America, he did not find the riches he was seeking. But he nonetheless accurately described the rugged, arid land he found, with scattered people speaking a babble of languages.

*Brass cross from Abó.*

To the Indians, Coronado and his companions definitely were from another world. Their language and culture were completely alien, and they brought with them metal, horses, and writing—all of which the Indians had never seen. Throughout the latter half of the sixteenth century, the people of the Estancia Basin must have heard many incredible stories of encounters with Spaniards. But no such encounter occurred in the basin itself until 1598.

To the small band of Spanish pioneers who trudged north in the spring of 1598, the New Mexico desert must have seemed like the end of the Earth. They were led by Don Juan de Oñate who, as *adelantado,* was entitled to advance the frontier. Behind them were weary weeks of sand and dry mountains, and it looked like more to come. With each rugged mile the fledgling colonists realized this effort would be hard, so far from the cultural hearth. The unknown circled all around, and the tracks back to New Spain were quickly erased by the afternoon winds.

From the early explorers Oñate had learned something about the Indians of New Mexico. Unlike the nomadic tribes the Spaniards had met in the south, the Indians in New Mexico were farmers who lived in towns. Therefore the Spanish word for town, "Pueblo," came to stand for both the various groups and the towns they lived in.

Determined to know more about the Pueblo Indians he viewed as now under his control, Oñate learned all he could from informants along the way. Soon after establishing a permanent camp near San Juan Pueblo, about forty miles north of present-day Santa Fe, he called the leaders of the Indian towns to a meeting. Chance encounters had taught a few Indians bits of Spanish, and various Indians spoke each other's languages, but still it must have been linguistic chaos.

Imagine Oñate's problems as he tried to issue *and translate* the "Act of Obedience" in the stately language of European conquest:

". . . render obedience and vassalage to God and king, and in their stead, to the most reverend father commissary in spiritual matters, and to the governor in temporal matters and those relating to the government of their public affairs." The Pueblos watched and listened, fascinated and overwhelmed by the wealth and magic of these strangers. With their horses, firearms, and wondrous metal armor, the Spaniards must have had connections to some very powerful gods.

In October 1598, Oñate finally saw the towns of the Estancia Basin for himself. Spanish bureaucrats were inveterate record keepers, so we even know the names of some Indians he met. "Ayquian" and "Aguim," their names inscribed phonetically in Spanish, made their marks on the Act of Obedience, on behalf of the Estancia Basin pueblo called Cuarac (Quarai). The date was October 12, 1598, 106 years to the day after Columbus' landfall. Five days later three other leaders signed for other nearby pueblos: Yolha for Cueloce (probably Las Humanas), Pocaetaqui (possibly for Pueblo Pardo, a small pueblo an hour's walk from Las Humanas), and Haye (perhaps for Tabirá, another pueblo near Las Humanas).

Persuading the pueblo leaders to sign the Act of Obedience was not all that was required to make a colony, and Oñate knew it. The Spanish crown hoped the New Mexico colony would thrive, producing agricultural products and even mineral wealth, if it could be found. It was difficult. Many of the pueblos, including those of the Estancia Basin, were far from Oñate's primitive adobe-and-wood bastion at San Juan, and travel was both difficult and dangerous. How could he govern them, and develop the economy the crown expected?

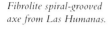

*Fibrolite spiral-grooved axe from Las Humanas.*

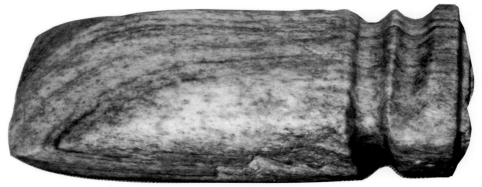

For years Oñate struggled to keep the enterprise together. In 1600 warriors from the Estancia Basin pueblo of Abó attacked a small band of soldiers and killed two who may have been deserters from the colony, returning to Mexico. Oñate responded in force, sending Captain Vicente de Zaldívar with troops, who in turn were attacked near Quarai. The battle turned against the Pueblos, whose wood and stone weapons were no match in hand-to-hand combat with the soldiers who had metal blades. The Indians retreated into their stone houses with wooden roofs, which the Spaniards set ablaze. It was not a good beginning.

The arid land of New Mexico was hard to farm, and alternatives were few. Still, under the Spanish system colonists were not free to come and go. They were in desolate New Mexico at the selection or direction of the crown, and could not leave without permission. There was bitterness when things did not go well.

Oñate recommended that the colony be abandoned and, from a purely economic point of view, that probably would have been the wisest thing to do. Spain was a worldly empire, with very real debts and contracts, vast lands to administer and a huge government to run. New Mexico was a drain on the royal treasury.

But Spain also was thoroughly, devoutly Catholic, and the Pope had made Spain responsible for converting the natives in the New World. Spanish colonial authority in New Mexico was vested in both the civil government, with Oñate as governor, and the Franciscan Order of the Holy Catholic Church. The Franciscans strongly pressed the case for the colony as a Pueblo Indian evangelization effort, and their argument prevailed with the King of Spain. Oñate resigned, disillusioned and broken.

So New Mexico essentially became a missionary colony. The missions were the principal extension of both the Catholic church and Spanish civilization, and the church was entitled to the protection and cooperation of the state. But church and state aims were frequently in conflict, and New Mexico was far from any central authority. The Franciscans were the only religious order in the colony, and usually spoke with one voice. They firmly believed the church's authority should supersede the state's. Predictably, the governor usually saw things differently.

24

*Steel lance or buffalo-spear point.*

To get for the crown what they considered to be the crown's, the Spanish civil government depended primarily upon the *encomienda*, or tribute, system. An individual judged worthy by the crown was entitled, as *encomendero*, to collect an annual tribute from a village. For example, the *encomienda* might be paid with goods, such as grain or *mantas* (woven blankets), produced by the village. In return, the *encomendero* was responsible for protecting the village from Apache raiders.

Under a different system, the *repartimiento*, Pueblo Indians were obliged to render tribute with their service, rather than goods. It was illegal to require both goods and service as tribute, although the law frequently was ignored.

The Act of Obedience put the Indians in a dilemma. On a given day the priest might demand that they pull weeds in the mission fields, while the *encomendero* pressured them for the annual tribute. Meanwhile the village fields were neglected, with no one available to do the work.

The colony was too distant, and too small, for the bureaucracy to inhibit individual ambitions. In New Mexico, months or years away from review by higher authorities, conflicts between civil and religious leaders were not always settled amicably.

For example, in 1613 Governor Pedro de Peralta sent soldiers to collect the tribute from Taos on a holy day, in open defiance of the priest who demanded that they stay in Santa Fe. Enraged at this blasphemous conceit, Fray Isidro Ordóñez, *custos* of the church, declared himself the agent of the much feared Inquisition, arrested Governor Peralta, and imprisoned him in his own colony. This bitter battle between church and state over colonial authority would continue, setting the tone for subsequent events in the basin.

Sometimes odd things are preserved in the historical record. In 1612, a Mexico City silversmith named Miguel de Torres received a contract to make seven silver chalices for some new missions on the New Mexico frontier. Those chalices cost the Franciscans 56 pesos each, but the real price would be paid by the Indians. The arrival of the Spanish missions would cost the Indians of the Estancia basin their way of life. Eventually, Indians and Spaniards alike would abandon the Estancia Basin completely.

25

By 1618 the Spaniards had established missions at most of the pueblos along the Rio Grande, especially those near the new capital of Santa Fe. Although the Franciscans had yet to venture into the Estancia Basin, a five-day walk from Santa Fe, people living in the basin must have heard about strange building activity in the Rio Grande Valley from travelers who passed from pueblo to pueblo, trading stories along with their wares. These Spaniards knew how to build awesome rooms, and they worshipped in these vast spaces with wonderful pomp and ceremony.

Other rumors were disturbing. The Spaniards expected the Indians to help build and maintain these missions, and toil in the fields, kitchens, and classrooms that supported them. In return the Indians had access to the new religion, which they surely hoped would supplement their ancient deities in these unprecedented times. They also learned Spanish traditions of farming and ranching, the latter being entirely new to people who had never seen a cow.

The Spaniards called the Estancia Basin the "Salinas Province," after the salines from which the Indians collected salt to trade to other pueblos and Spaniards alike. The first Spaniard to actually take up permanent residence in the Salinas Province was a man of the cloth, Fray Alonso de Peinado, who had been in charge of the Franciscans in New Mexico in the early years and had founded the mission at Santo Domingo. Peinado had become fed up with incessant church-state infighting, so in 1618 he banished himself to distant Chililí, an Indian village north of Quarai, to convert the Indians there. Four years later, another priest, Fray Francisco Fonte, arrived at the thriving Indian town of Abó to build the basin's first mission there.

*Section Five*

# BUILDING THE CHURCHES

The mission system in New Mexico was supported by church-administered supply trains that made the months-long, arduous haul from Mexico City to Santa Fe every three years. Accompanied by a herd of cattle, whose constant bawling was punctuated by the "crack!" of bullwhips, this triennial caravan brought new priests and supplies to the growing network of missions.

Packed in those wagons were containers of lamp oil for altars yet to be built, in churches yet to be designed, in pueblos yet to host their first Spaniard. One marvels at the confidence with which these missionaries set out, and the extent to which they succeeded. A partial list of initial supplies assigned to each friar hints at the enormity of the challenge, and the sheer physical labor involved in establishing a mission on the frontier:

*10 axes*
*10 hoes*
*1 medium-sized saw*
    *[plus chisels, augers, a box plane for smoothing boards]*
*600 tinned nails [for decorating the church door]*
*60 nails four inches long   [other nail sizes, counts]*
*10 pounds of steel for making other tools*
*1 large latch for the church door*
*12 hinges*

There were personal items, and sacred supplies:

*Complete set of vestments [minimum 5 pieces]*
*Rug for altar steps*
*[various cloths, such as damask & Rouen]*
*Enameled silver chalice*
*One small bell to sound the Sanctus*
*One pair brass candlesticks*
*One pair snuffing scissors*
*One copper vessel for holy water*
*One wafer box for the unconsecrated host*
*Two and a half pounds of incense*
*Three ounces silk wicking to make candles*
*Three peso's worth of soap for washing vestments*
*Missal, three books of chants*

The contract promised some renewables every three years:

*45 gallons sacramental wine*
*42 pounds of prepared candle wax*
*26 gallons lamp oil for illuminating the altar*

*Spanish metal tools.*

Upon arriving at Abó, Fray Francisco Fonte first negotiated with the village leaders, and either purchased or was given several rooms on the outside edge of one of the room blocks. Almost certainly he converted one of them to a temporary chapel. Fonte then turned to more ambitious aims.

Fonte knew what a mission should look like, in principle. Years of training had exposed him to many churches in Spain, Mexico and the colonial hinterlands. Theologically and practically, he knew what the basic requirements were. New Mexico missions built during the seventeenth century shared certain characteristics, but the buildings also displayed intriguing individuality, showing that they did not come from standardized plans. The architectural and engineering skills of these priest-builders were remarkable. They knew the forces and weights involved in large-scale buildings, and often devised sophisticated solutions.

The mission was more than just a church building. The Franciscans also taught the Indians the Spanish language, new agricultural methods, and crafts. A *convento* was needed to house this effort. For the *convento* at Abó, Fonte laid out two large connected square buildings with rows of rooms surrounding two *garths* (open courtyards). The *convento* contained a dining room, kitchen, storerooms, infirmary, latrine, classrooms, storerooms, workshops, and sleeping rooms for the religious. Fonte and helpers pegged out the plan on the ground with surveying tools, then Indian laborers dug the foundation trenches.

*Though most have been replaced, this is an original beam at Quarai.*

The red Abó sandstone, which broke in roughly tabular pieces, was well suited for wall construction, and there was plenty of clay and water for mortar. The Pueblos had centuries of experience in this type of construction, and the women and children soon erected the walls. Timbers brought from the mountains were laid across the walls as vigas. Smaller sticks, brush, and dirt completed the roofs. The building's dimensions, including doors and windows, were larger than the Pueblo people were accustomed to, but the building techniques were familiar.

If the size of the *convento* impressed the Indians, the church Fonte laid out must have astonished them. He planned a building about twenty-five feet wide and eighty-four feet long on the inside, with a ceiling over twenty-five feet high.

As the walls rose other crews began the timber work, thankful that the Spaniards had brought metal axes, an incredible advance over the stone tools the Pueblos had. In addition to creating scaffolds for the masonry crews, Pueblo woodworkers learned to make window frames, doors, and stairs. One set of stairs led to the choir loft, while another was needed to reach and ring the two-hundred-pound stationary bell in the tower.

Large logs for ceiling beams had to be cut, trimmed, carried from the mountains, and carved before being lifted into place. Today empty beam sockets still hold scraps of plaster displaying the negative mold of the original carved beams. Lifting the beams twenty-five feet high was a difficult and sometimes dangerous job. Shear-jacks, the x-shaped hoists used on Spanish ships, probably were devised to lift the beams into position.

29

Fonte made the roof above the transept and altar a few feet higher than the roof over the nave, where the people stood, and installed an opening called a clerestory window in the space between the two roof levels. This window, not visible to the congregation, focused a dramatic beam of light on the altar and the decorations around it.

In 1626 Fray Alonso de Benavides, the dynamic new *custos* for New Mexico, arrived on the mission supply train with twelve new priests and plans to build a burst of new missions. Benavides's responsibilities included the Salinas Province, and he assigned fellow-traveler Fray Juan Gutiérrez de la Chica to establish a mission at Quarai.

The following year Gutiérrez began construction on Nuestra Señora de la Purísima Concepción de Cuarac (Quarai). He chose to build the mission on a large mound of abandoned rooms on the east side of the village. After first constructing a retaining wall around the mound, he and his Pueblo laborers leveled the rubble within.

*Plans for the never-completed second church at Mission San Buena-ventura, Las Humanas, embodied the classic elements of Spanish mission architecture.*

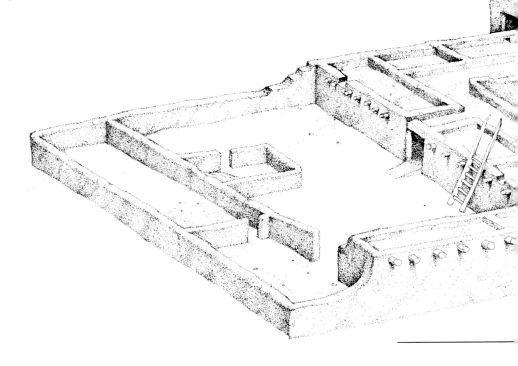

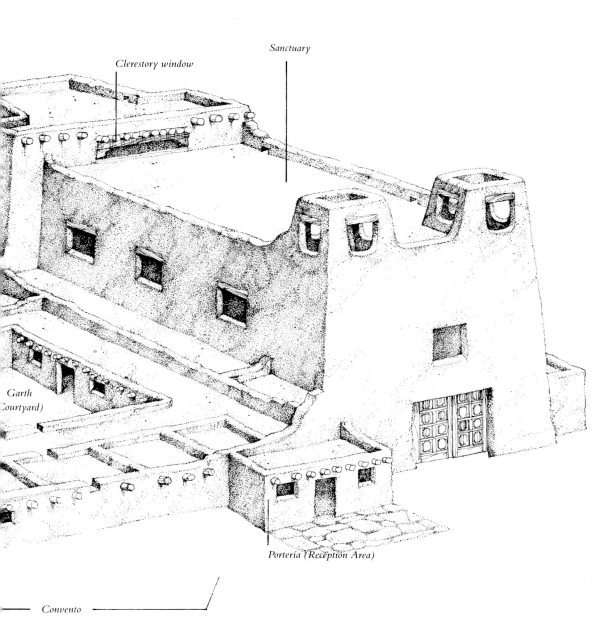

Clerestory window

Sanctuary

Garth
(Courtyard)

Porteria (Reception Area)

Convento

31

The people of Quarai first built the *convento* before tackling Gutiérrez's ambitious design for the church itself, which was to form the shape of a cross and be considerably larger than the one Fonte had just completed at Abó. On a foundation 7 feet deep and 6 feet wide, the workmen constructed 5-foot-thick walls as high as 40 feet, enclosing a space that was 100 feet long, with a 27-foot-wide nave and 50-foot-wide transept. It took five years for the skilled Pueblo laborers to produce one of the grandest churches on the frontier.

Before these missions were built, few Indians had ever seen an enclosed volume greater than their own rooms and kivas, which were quite small by comparison. Imagine their sense of accomplishment and wonder as they worshiped in these great sanctuaries they built to the glory of this new religion.

A governor once complained that the church buildings the Franciscans built were too elaborate. He insisted that, if a person truly worshiped, a hut would do. He found himself summoned before the Inquisition, which held that noble architecture and pageantry were essential and effective in converting the Pueblos.

Today, on rare mornings when fog covers the Salinas, one can hear clear echoes in the now-roofless churches. Imagine what it must have been like for Pueblo Indians of the seventeenth century to walk into these sanctuaries for the first time.

*Las Humanas pueblo in foreground, in front of the second church at Mission San Buenaventura.*

*Rainbow at sunset over Abó.*

*Mission Nuestra Señora de la Purísima Concepción de Cuarac.*

*Convento walls at Las Humanas.*

*Mission San Gregorio de Abó.*

*Convento walls of Mission San Buenaventura, Gran Quivira.*

Benavides himself visited the Salinas Province in 1627 and "accomplished the conversion" of Las Humanas. Today, at the Gran Quivira Unit of Salinas Pueblo Missions National Monument, the visitor trail leads through a large plaza between house mounds, past what appears to be the circular remains of a large kiva. Apparently this was the main plaza where Benavides stood on April 4, 1627, and preached to the natives. He described the day in his *Memorial* to Pope Urban III three years later:

*I was in the middle of the plaza, preaching to numerous persons assembled there, and this old sorcerer, realizing that my arguments were having some effect on the audience, descended from a corridor with an infuriated and wicked disposition, and said to me, 'You Christians are crazy, you desire and intend that this pueblo shall also be crazy." I asked him in what respect we were crazy. He had been, no doubt, in some Christian pueblo during Holy Week when they were flagellating themselves in procession and thus he answered me, 'How are you crazy? You go through the streets in groups, flagellating yourselves, and it is not well that the people of the pueblo should commit such madness as spilling their own blood by scourging themselves.' When he saw that I laughed, as did those around me, he rushed out of the pueblo, saying that he did not wish to be crazy. When I explained to the people the reason why we scourged ourselves, they laughed all the more at the old man and were more confirmed in their desire to become Christians.*

The Indian priest expressed quite logical doubts about what he had seen adherents of this new religion do, and the subtleties of Benavides's explanation may not have survived the translation. Benavides also claimed his sermon was so effective that a great number of Indians embraced the new faith immediately, and rejected their old religion. More likely, the polytheistic Indians saw this new god as a logical addition to the ones they already had. After all, they had borrowed effective deities from neighboring peoples before.

Much of this new religion rang true to the Pueblos. The Bible stories were set in a desert land, to which the Pueblos could relate. When the people heard how Elijah competed with the prophets of Baal to see who could break the drought, it made sense. These were real problems that needed real solutions.

(left) *Bell tower of Mission San Gregorio de Abó.*

41

From the Indians' point of view, a kiva and a church could be perfectly harmonious. Indeed, at both the Abó and Quarai missions there appears to be a kiva in the *garth*, or courtyard, of each *convento*. The Franciscans should have considered such a thing to be sacrilegious, but perhaps they pragmatically allowed the kivas to be built to help the Indians make the transition to Christianity. In any event, mass conversions such as Benavides recorded almost always failed, as each side gradually realized what the other side *really* meant.

Among the new priests who arrived on the 1629 supply train were Fray Francisco Acevedo, who was assigned to assist Fonte at Abó, and Fray Francisco Letrado, who began the church at Las Humanas.

Like Fray Fonte at Abó, Letrado took over eight abandoned Indian rooms, which were later unearthed by archeologist Alden Hayes. Letrado remodeled the rooms and there is evidence he widened the original, tiny doorways, perhaps to better accommodate the skirts of his Franciscan habit. Letrado changed one room into a small chapel, and his first mass in this remote place must have fascinated his hosts.

When the temporary facilities were ready, Letrado next planned a large, permanent church building and *convento*. It took considerable effort to cut into the hillside at what would become the altar end of the church, using the dirt and rock as fill at the other end. Letrado had just begun work on the walls when, in the autumn of 1631, he was transferred at his request to Zuni.

Tragically, Letrado was martyred there the following spring. It appears that he may have interrupted an Indian ceremony to urge the people to mass. The affront was fatal. A military force was sent from Santa Fe to exact retribution, and during a rest-and-water stop at the rock called "El Morro" the troop marked their passing, as so many other travelers had done, by carving graffiti into the soft sandstone cliff.

When Letrado left Las Humanas he was not replaced. Acevedo supervised completion of the small church, visible at the Gran Quivira unit of the park today, but the village could not support a major mission. All missions, including those in the Salinas, were expected to establish large-scale farming and ranching operations to

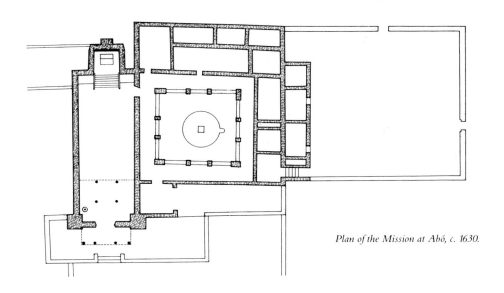

*Plan of the Mission at Abó, c. 1630.*

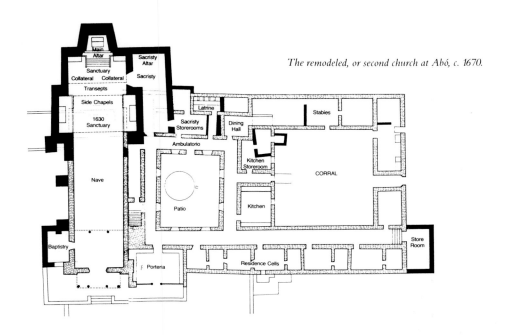

*The remodeled, or second church at Abó, c. 1670.*

Main Altar

Sanctuary

Sacristy Altar

Collateral    Collateral

Sacristy

Transepts

Side Chapels

1630 Sanctuary

Latrine

Stables

Sacristy Storerooms

Dining Hall

Ambulatorio

Kitchen Storeroom

Nave

CORRAL

Patio

Kitchen

Baptistry

Store Room

Porteria

Residence Cells

help defray operating costs and teach the Pueblo people Spanish agricultural techniques. But farming and ranching of any sort requires water, and Las Humanas barely had enough to live on. The churches at Las Humanas and Tabirá, another village not within the boundaries of the present-day park, thus became *visitas,* or circuit parishes, which Acevedo served from Abó.

In 1640, after eleven years under Fonte's tutelage, Acevedo became the sole guardian at Abó, and began to renovate and enlarge the buildings there almost immediately. It was a remarkable job of designing and planning, both to use the aging church as the basis for the new one, and to arrange construction so the *convento* and church could continue to be used during construction.

First, the north, altar end was removed entirely. Then the roof was dismantled, probably with much advice from old workmen who remembered hoisting the heavy timbers the first time. Workmen built buttresses on the outside of both side walls to support them while the roof was absent.

Next, the altar end was rebuilt and a new, higher roof constructed. This was no minor task. The main vigas were about forty-six feet long, weighed about 1,700 pounds each, and had to be lifted more than thirty-four feet and carefully placed. The interior was plastered and painted, and new altars and other furnishings were built and installed. It took about six years for Acevedo to complete San Gregorio de Abó, one of the most remarkable churches in the New Mexico colony.

*Section Six*

# LIFE IN A MISSION

(above) *Tabirá Polychrome olla from Las Humanas.*

Fray Benavides's *Memorial* to Pope Urban III, describing the missions in New Mexico in 1630, offers an intriguing look at everyday mission life in the seventeenth century, or at least a Spanish priest's rosy version of it. Benavides described a program for which he himself was responsible, and he had unquestioned faith in the church and its role in this remote corner of the empire. But he made no attempt to chronicle events from the Indians' point of view.

Benavides's patronizing account belies the fact that the villages of the Salinas had existed for centuries before the Spaniards arrived, and the people had developed a religion and a culture that were rich and inseparable. Furthermore, the Pueblo people lived only slightly above a subsistence level when the Spaniards arrived, and each person already was fully involved in the maintenance of the village. With the additional work required to build and sustain the missions, something had to give.

*Since the land is very remote and isolated and the difficulties of the long journeys require more than a year of travel, the friars, although there are many who wish to dedicate themselves to those conversions, find themselves unable to do so because of their poverty. Hence, only those who go there are sent by the Catholic King, at his own expense, for the cost is too excessive that only his royal zeal can afford it. This is the reason that there are few friars over there and that most of the convents have only one religious each,*

45

and he ministers to four, six, or more neighboring pueblos, in the midst of which he stands as a lighted torch to guide them in spiritual as well as temporal affairs. More than twenty Indians, devoted to the service of the church, live with him in a convent. They take turns in relieving one another as porters, sextons, cooks, bell-ringers, gardeners, refectioners, and in other tasks. They perform their duties with as much circumspection and care as if they were friars. At eventide, they say their prayers together, with much devotion, in front of some image.

In every pueblo where a friar resides, he has schools for the teaching of praying, singing, playing musical instruments and other interesting things. Promptly at dawn, one of the Indian singers, whose turn it is that week, goes

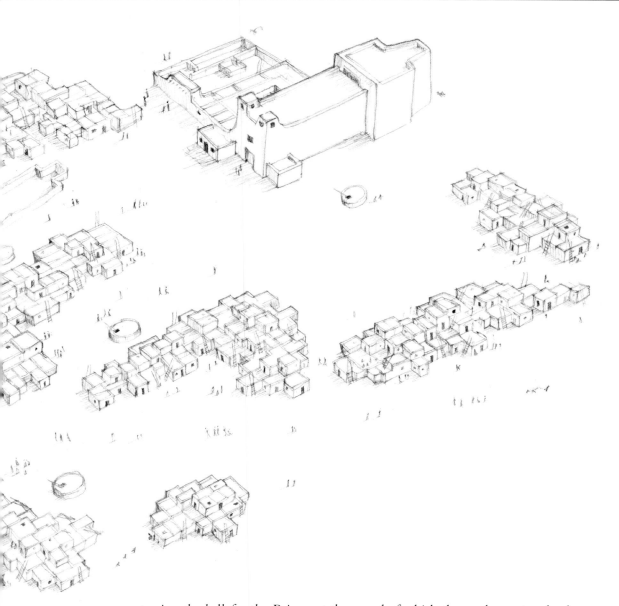

*Artist's conception of Pueblo de Las Humanas.*

to ring the bell for the Prime, at the sound of which those who go to school assemble and sweep the rooms thoroughly. The singers chant the Prime in the choir. The friar must be present at all of this and takes note of those who have failed to perform this duty, in order to reprimand them later. When everything is neat and clean, they again ring the bell and each one goes to *learn his particular specialty; the friar oversees it all, in order that these students may be mindful of what they are doing. At this time those who plan to get married come and notify him, so that he may prepare and instruct them according to our holy council; if there are any, either sick or healthy persons, who wish to confess in order to receive communion at mass, or who wish anything else, they come to tell him. After they have been occupied in this manner for an hour and a half, the bell is rung for mass. All go into the church, and the friar says mass and administers the sacraments. Mass over, they gather in different groups, examine the lists, and take note of those who are absent in order to reprimand them later. After taking the roll, all kneel down by the church door and sing the Salve in their own tongue. This concluded, the friar says: "Praised be the most Holy Sacrament," and dismisses them, warning them first of the circumstances with which they should go about their daily business.*

*At mealtime, the poor people in the pueblo who are not ill come to the porter's lodge, where the cooks of the convent have sufficient food ready, which is served to them by the friars; food for the sick is sent to their homes. After mealtime, it always happens that the friar has to go to some neighboring pueblo to hear a confession or to see if they are careless in the boys' school, where they learn to pray and assist at mass for this is the responsibility of the sextons and it is their duty always to have a dozen boys for the service of the sacristy and to teach them how to help at mass and how to pray.*

*In the evening, they toll the bell for vespers, which are chanted by the singers who are on duty for the week, and, according to the importance of the feast, they celebrate it with organ chants as they do for mass. Again the friar supervises and looks after everything, the same as in the morning.*

*On feast days, he says mass in the pueblo very early, and administers the sacraments and preaches. Then he goes to say a second mass in another pueblo, whose turn it is, where he observes the same procedure, and then he returns to his convent. These two masses are attended by the people of the tribe, according to their proximity to the pueblo where they are celebrated.*

*One of the weekdays which is not so busy is devoted to baptism and all those who are to be baptized come to the church on that day, unless some urgent matter should intervene; in that case, it is performed at any time.*

*With great care, their names are inscribed in a book; in another, those who are married; and in another, the dead.*

*One of the greatest tasks of the friars is to adjust the disputes of the Indians among themselves, for since they look upon him as a father, they come to him with all their troubles, and he has to take pains to harmonize them. If it is a question of land and property, he must go with them and mark their boundaries, and thus pacify them.*

*For the support of all the poor of the pueblo, the friar makes them sow some grain and raise some cattle, because if he left it to their discretion, they would not do anything. Therefore, the friar requires them to do so and trains them so well that with the meat he feeds all the poor and pays the various workmen who come to build the churches. With the wool he clothes all the poor, and the friar himself also gets his clothing and food from this source. All the wheels of this clock must be kept in good order by the friar, without neglecting any detail, otherwise all would be totally lost.*

*The most important thing is the good example set by the friars. This, aside from the obligations of their vows, is forced upon them because they live in a province where they concern themselves with nothing but God. Death stares them in the face everyday! Today one of their companions is martyred, tomorrow, another; their hope is that such a good fortune may befall them while living a perfect life.*

Benavides gets high marks from historians, a good man striving in challenging circumstances. But the Pueblos might have argued with his assessment of them. Those twenty Indians who lived in the mission certainly had to forego the responsibilities of traditional family and village life. They were not available to do the chores, as they would have been before. The amount of work and classroom and ceremonial time required of the Pueblos was enormous, and involved far

*Franciscan friar.*

49

more than the twenty individuals who happened to live in the *convento*. The circumspection with which the Indians performed their tasks may have been the result, rather than the cause, of frequent "reprimanding."

Benavides expressed concern that the Indians did not grow as many crops as he thought they should, but archeologists' counts of animal bones at the site reveal that the people of the Salinas previously depended on hunting and gathering for perhaps 50 percent of their diet. This was not reflected in the priests' calculations. Finally, by intervening to settle property disputes, the priest tore the very fabric of traditional village structure. Small wonder Letrado was not the only priest to be martyred.

*Section Seven*

# THE CHURCH
# AND STATE IN CONFLICT

(above) *Tiwa Red soup plate, a pottery form introduced by the Spanish, found in a kiva at Abó.*

The conflicts between the Indians and the Spanish friars were exacerbated by the ongoing battle between the civil and religious Spanish authorities. The only exploitable resources in New Mexico, for the governor's gang and the friars alike, were the Indians. The Franciscans saw gold in Indian souls, while the king's men demanded their labor.

This frontier did not attract the cream of the mother society, but rather the disinherited, people who in many cases were escaping the law or debts. For them, the risks of life on the frontier were infinitely preferable to the certainty of their miserable lot elsewhere in the empire. For soldiers it was a punitive assignment.

What would compel a senior diplomat, or a successful merchant or artist, to want to be sent to distant, dangerous New Mexico? A "comer" in court, or a rising government official, might seek the governorship of New Mexico as a stepping stone, but it was not a "plum," like those available in the Philippines or Peru.

The governor had only a few years to glean what he could from this remote assignment, before the dreaded day when his successor began the *residencia*, or review of his administration. The review was unlikely to be fair. Each succeeding governor brought a "What's in it for me?" mentality to the job, and used the *residencia* to filch a piece of his predecessor's pie. Usually this was accomplished by means of a fine, levied for transgressions real or imagined.

51

Governor Juan de Eulate, who served from 1618 to 1625, and many other Spaniards dealt in Indian slaves, usually Apaches. The practice had a slight legal veneer. The law allowed Spaniards to acquire Indians "orphaned" through warfare. These orphans were to be taken in, raised in a Spanish home, and given the advantages of Christianity and Spanish culture. But the system was widely abused. Domestic servants were obtained this way, and many slaves were exported to Mexico.

The booming silver mines of Parral in northern Mexico needed two things the New Mexico colony could supply: salt and slaves. The Salinas Pueblo Indians were required under the *repartimiento* system to collect salt from the salines of long-dead Lake Estancia, even as the Spaniards rounded up and enslaved neighboring Apaches.

The soul of an Apache was just as valuable in God's sight as the soul of a Pueblo, but in New Mexico there were so few missionaries and so many Indians. The Pueblos, at least, lived in towns like "civilized" people. Surely the Franciscans would have liked to minister to the Apaches, as well. But how could the church establish a mission to the fearsome Apaches, who were always on the move?

The priests who ministered to the Pueblos appeared to look the other way while the secular Spaniards attacked and captured Apaches. The distinction between sacred and secular was lost on the Apaches, to whom a Spaniard was a Spaniard, any Spaniard was an enemy, and a friend of the enemy became an enemy, too. Apaches, who historically had maintained a good trading relationship with the Pueblos, increased their raiding and the cycle of violence continued.

Many governors exhibited an entrepreneurial flair. For example, in 1637 Governor Luis de las Rosas established workshops in Santa Fe where Pueblos from the Salinas area, as well as Apache slaves, labored on goods for him to sell in Mexico. He also raided the plains to capture slaves he apparently had already contracted to deliver in Mexico.

The empty wagons of the mission supply trains were often commandeered by the governors to haul goods south for sale in Parral or Chihuahua City. Return cargos included coarse and tailored woolen cloth, blankets, drapes, buffalo and antelope skins, pinyon nuts, candles, and leather bags of salt, which were packed through Abó Pass from the Estancia Basin. The wagons that brought priests to save Indian souls also returned to Mexico with Indian slaves. This particularly enraged the Franciscans, who had contracted for the use of the wagons in the first place.

The conflict between church and state in New Mexico came to a head during the controversial tenure of Governor Don Bernardo López de Mendizábal. He earned the enmity of the Franciscans before he even arrived in 1660, and ultimately he and his subordinates would be called before the Inquisition to answer a long list of charges stemming from his brief administration. Trial records provide invaluable insight into life in the Salinas during the early 1660s.

The replacement priests who traveled with López on the mission supply train noted he did not seem to have the proper respect for the church. Rarely did he or his wife leave their wagon for mass during the journey. Once they had the wagon placed so they could hear the mass without having to emerge. Flippant comments the governor made toward the church were documented.

On a later inspection trip to the Salinas pueblos Governor López held a forum and plainly invited the Indians to register any complaints they had against the priests. Someone accused aged Acevedo, who had built the great church at Abó, of sexual impropriety. The accusation itself, and the fact the governor countenanced it, infuriated the priests.

Word quickly spread among the Franciscans that the governor had told Indians they no longer had to obey the priests. The governor likely wanted the support of the Pueblos for economic reasons, and therefore told them to ignore religious obligations that might interfere with their working for him. To the priests, this constituted an outrageous attack on theology.

One of López's first acts as governor was to appoint Nicolás de Aguilar *alcalde mayor* of the Salinas Province to manage civil affairs there. A typical frontier character, Aguilar was at home with rough and tumble ways. He had worked in the tough mining towns of New Spain as a youth, and circumstances later brought him to New Mexico. Very much the governor's man, he gave lip service to the sanctity of the church.

Aguilar agreed heartily when the governor attempted to ease restrictions priests had placed on Pueblo ceremonies, the most visible being the kachina dances, in which Indians costumed as spiritual figures danced in the plazas. To the Franciscans the dances were demonic, but Governor López and Aguilar enjoyed their boisterous joviality. Far from condemning the native dances and music, Aguilar was heard to mutter that the Indian chanting "had no more effect than the Gregorian chants of the Fathers." The priests were outraged when Governor López officially allowed the dances again, and even invited Pueblos to dance on the plaza in Santa Fe, before the Palace of the Governors.

In 1659 Las Humanas received a new priest and was upgraded from *visita* to mission again. The new priest, Fray Diego de Santander, initiated construction of a huge new church to replace the small one Letrado had begun and Acevedo had finished. During construction, word spread that the Indians had been forbidden to assist him. The governor and Aguilar denied it.

In connection with this argument over Indian labor, the subject of Las Humanas' poor water supply surfaced. Water had to be carried to the mission herd, so the governor ordered the herd moved to Abó, which had a greater water supply. The church, of course, saw this as an attack on its affairs.

The priests also claimed Aguilar once ordered twenty Indians at Quarai whipped "because they went to the pueblo of the Jumanos [Las Humanas] to sing in the choir during the celebration of the feast of San Buenaventura." In his defense, Aguilar explained that he punished the Quarai choir for violating a peace accord he had made with the Apaches. Quarai guards had once inadvertently killed two Apaches who were on their way to Las Humanas to trade. Aguilar had pursuaded the Apaches the killings were accidental, and got the Apaches to agree not to venture north of Las Humanas toward Quarai. In exchange, he promised the Pueblos of Quarai would not go to Las Humanas when Apaches were there to trade.

Fray Antonio Aguado, guardian of Abó, required a translator because he could not speak the Indian language. He accused Aguilar of ordering the translator not to enter the *convento*, on pain of being whipped two hundred lashes. Aguilar claimed he made the threat because the man had bullied other Indians, and certainly did not intend to inconvenience Aguado.

Aguilar once interrupted a sermon preached at Quarai by Friar Nicolás de Freitas, who was emphasizing the supreme role of God and the church and the necessity of the Indians' obedience. Aguilar declared that no, the Pueblos owed allegiance to the king. It became a shouting match, in the church! Freitas stormed out to his quarters in the *convento*, and Aguilar followed, still arguing. The Indians observed everything.

Pottery candlestick, Las Humanas.

Aguilar and the priests repeatedly clashed over the use of Indian labor. Aguilar once forced an Indian woman who cooked for the mission to leave, because women were not permitted to enter the *convento*. When Aguilar forbade the Pueblo people from going to the mountains to gather firewood, citing the risk of attack by Apaches, Fray Fernando de Velasco persisted and sent them anyway. Aguilar had the Indians whipped for disobeying, and Velasco publicly berated Aguilar, calling him "a Calvinist heretic, a Lutheran, and other names of heretics." Witnesses claimed the enraged Velasco actually tried to stab Aguilar.

At Las Humanas, Fray Diego de Santander complained that some of the Indians were careless about attending mass. Aguilar replied that the Indians might not know much about the faith, but they certainly knew "how to guard and herd an infinite number of livestock, to serve as slaves, and to fill barns with grain, cultivated and harvested with their blood, not for their humble homes, but for those of the friars."

When a Salinas man and woman were sent to Aguilar for punishment for an illicit sexual union, he ascertained they were both single, and wanted to marry. He allowed them to do so, judging it a better solution than whipping them.

On another occasion, it was the priest at the Salinas village of Tajique, Fray Diego de Parraga, who was accused of having had a three-year illicit relationship with an Indian's wife. Aguilar assembled people who might be witnesses, and in the process he asked them questions about the case. A legal uproar resulted when this prior questioning was disclosed at the hearing. By what right did a civil officer, an *alcalde mayor*, investigate the clergy? Was that not the

55

clergy's sole right? Who had ordered what? Had the proper papers been signed? On May 29, 1660, Nicolás de Aguilar was declared excommunicate from the church for violating ecclesiastical immunity, and for showing a lack of respect for the censures of the church.

At the end of his term, Governor López was replaced by Don Diego Dionisio de Peñalosa Briceño y Berdugo, who held a *residencia*. Eventually López, Aguilar, and others were arrested and taken to Mexico City to be tried before the Holy Tribunal of the Inquisition. López died awaiting trial, but on May 8, 1663, Aguilar was read an indictment containing fifty-two articles, including those above, stemming from his administration of the Salinas Province.

Aguilar defended himself vigorously. Did obeying the order of a superior constitute a defense? Which evidence was circumstantial, which direct? Which actions were proper for civil authorities, and which for religious authorities?

In September 1664 Aguilar was found guilty, and he appealed. After three months of reconsideration the final verdict was upheld, and the punishment made more severe. Aguilar was banished from New Mexico for ten years, and barred from administrative office for life. In December this miner, rancher, politician, and instrument of chaos in the Salinas Province admitted and rejected his errors, and was released.

*Section Eight*

# DROUGHT, FAMINE AND DEPARTURE

(above) *Lizard effigy found at Las Humanas.*

In the spring of 1661 the Franciscan *custos*, Fray Alonso de Posada, ordered priests throughout the colony to confiscate the ceremonial equipment of the Pueblos, and in many instances to destroy the kivas. At Las Humanas, all seven kivas dating from that period show evidence that they were destroyed, and some archeologists believe excavation of other sites would reveal the same.

This failed to crush the religion, for near each deliberately destroyed kiva, in interior pueblo rooms where priests were not likely to venture, ceremonial goods have been found. Some of these room walls were painted, as kivas often were. The Pueblos kept their faith alive by moving their ceremonies inside, beyond the eyes of the priests. It was vital for the Pueblos to perform those ceremonies. They needed all the help they could get to face drought, disease, forced labor, Apache depredations, and famine.

When times got hard, the Spaniards pushed harder. Routine tasks of supporting the missions were demanding enough for the Pueblos. Occasional special tasks only added to their crushing work load.

Sixty men from Quarai were once forced to carry loads of pinyon nuts from Las Humanas through Abó Pass to the Rio Grande, for seventeen days straight. Who took care of their fields while they were gone? And who collected the pinyon nuts in the first place? It took nineteen Indians from Abó to carry corn from Las

57

Humanas to Aguilar's house near Tajique. Then, twenty-two Indians from the village of Galisteo were sent to pick up the corn and take it to Santa Fe.

The governors frequently criticized the Franciscans for collecting huge stores of grain, but the priests argued they were needed for times of famine. Indeed, in the 1660s and 1670s even nature conspired against the province. Drought came. Wise men among the Pueblos were not surprised, as the traditional ceremonies had been performed poorly, or sometimes not at all.

Unrelenting hot days withered the spirit along with the tiny corn plants. In the old days the Indians usually could store enough corn to survive times of minimal or failed crops, but that was before there were so many newcomer mouths to feed. Rage increased when Spanish cattle broke into fields and grazed on the Pueblos' winter food.

It was in the midst of this drought that Fray Diego de Santander decided to build a new, larger church at Las Humanas. Apparently Santander finished the *convento* area, but he and his successor would lose the race to finish the sanctuary before the last hours of the province.

When famine was at its painful worst, Santander remodeled the kitchen and pantry to safely store what food was left. Santander had workmen create an interior, basement room which was accessible only through the *convento*. The room had no outside door at all, only a trap door with a ladder leading to an equally inaccessible room above. All this was immediately next to the kitchen.

Drought affected the surrounding Apaches, as well. Raids on the pueblos increased, and precious dwindling stores of food were stolen, adding to the misery of the violent raids themselves. In 1669 Fray Juan Bernal described the situation in a desperate letter: "One of these calamities is that the whole land is at war with the widespread heathen nation of the Apache Indians, who kill all the Christian Indians they can find. No road is safe; everyone travels at the risk of his life, for the heathen traverse them all, being courageous and brave. They hurl themselves at danger like people who know no God nor that there is any hell."

Disease rode the back of famine, and it subjected the subsistence Pueblo culture to horrendous mortality. Bernal's letter continues: "The second calamity is that for three years no crop has been harvested. Last year, 1668, a great many Indians perished of hunger, lying dead along the roads, in the ravines, and in their hovels. There were pueblos, like Las Humanas, where more than four hundred and fifty died of hunger. The same calamity still prevails, for, because there is no money, there is not a *fanega* of maize or wheat in all the kingdom. As a result the Spaniards, men as well as women, have sustained themselves for two years on the cowhides they have in their houses to sit on. They roast them and eat them. And the greatest woe of all is that they can no longer find a bit of leather to eat."

Food that Indian labor had produced and the missionaries had hoarded finally had to be used to supplement the meager stores in the villages. For instance, in the summer of 1672 at Abó Fray Gil de Ávila distributed more than two tons of corn, meat from thirty-seven sheep and twelve cows, plus seed corn that would later sprout and shrivel. The mission also supplied the governor's military detachment stationed nearby. The drought persisted, even after the storerooms were empty, and hundreds of people starved to death.

That same year a remarkable Salinas Pueblo leader named Don Esteban Clemente, who could both read and write Spanish, plotted a revolt. He planned to have Pueblo herders drive the Spaniards' horses to the mountains. Then they would attack and kill every Spaniard in the colony on the night of Holy Thursday. But the plot was discovered and Clemente was hanged.

It was hunger that finally drove the Spaniards — and the Indians — from the Salinas. Las Humanas was abandoned first, in 1671. The few surviving Indians probably went to Abó, or joined their linguistic cousins in the Rio Grande Valley. Fray Joseph de Paredes was the priest at Las Humanas at the abandonment, and he must have gone north toward either Abó or Quarai. As he reached the crest of a small rise about five miles north of Las Humanas, Paredes probably looked back one last time to see the massive walls of the uncompleted second church.

*Tabirá Black-on-white canteen, Las Humanas.*

59

By 1673 the storerooms at Abó were empty, and either Apaches or the Pueblos themselves burned the *convento*. Ávila fled, and the pueblo was soon abandoned. The calamity continued for Ávila, who joined the fight against the famine at the Rio Grande pueblo of Senecú but was killed in the *convento* there by Indians in an uprising in the winter of 1675.

Quarai, with its springs, lasted longest, but was abandoned by 1677. Today the departing view of the red sandstone church is obscured by greenery, but in 1677 there probably wasn't much, even at the head of the springs. Most likely the surviving Indians went north, into the Galisteo basin, surprisingly taking with them the remains of a long-buried, favorite priest, Fray Jer'onimo de la Llana.

The rest of the colony, Pueblos and Spaniards alike, absorbed the refugees from the desolated Salinas Province, leaving no one to hear the creak of roofs slowly collapsing, and no one to brush out the sand that blew into abandoned doorways. The Salinas became as quiet as when it had been a lake, so many centuries before.

*Section Nine*

# EPILOGUE

The abandonment of the Salinas foreshadowed the calamity that ultimately would overwhelm the rest of the colony. In the heat of August 1680, the Pueblos attacked in force. Blood flowed at isolated Spanish settlements throughout the colony, and at the remaining missions too.

In Santa Fe, the Pueblos lay siege to Spaniards who had taken refuge in the old adobe Palace of the Governors. After fierce fighting in the palace plaza, the grieving Spanish remnant straggled down the Rio Grande, joining refugees from the Salinas missions and the southern part of the colony. When they were far south, beyond the reach of the enraged and temporarily unified Pueblos, the Spanish refugees set up a semi-permanent camp at the crossing of the Rio Grande called "the Pass to the North"—"El Paso del Norte." The uprising was startlingly successful.

Twelve years later Don Diego de Vargas led the Reconquest of New Mexico. Lessons were learned from the painful experience of the seventeenth century. This time, Spain adopted much more "live-and-let-live" policies toward the Indians. Indian culture, including religious ceremonies, were tolerated as Spain attempted to better integrate New Mexico into the empire. Spain needed New Mexico, if for no other reason than to serve as a buffer against other European powers, whose empires in North America were rapidly expanding toward Spain's possessions.

61

Spaniards filtered north and reoccupied the scattered settlements in the Rio Grande Valley, but the increasing presence of Apaches delayed resettlement of the Salinas. Apaches traveled freely through the unprotected old Salinas Province, using Abó Pass to launch raids on pueblos and Spanish settlements along the Rio Grande.

In 1750 Governor Tomás Vélez Cachupín sent detachments of Spanish and Pueblo soldiers into the abandoned province to hinder the Apache raids. The small bands of troops temporarily reoccupied the slowly crumbling old missions of Quarai and Abó, both of which had springs and were close to travel routes. Waterless Las Humanas was too isolated to be of strategic importance.

The Pueblo people never returned to the Salinas, and not until the early nineteenth century did Spaniards begin to trickle back to stay. Lured by the empty farmlands, Miguel Lucero and his family settled near Quarai. Working with one eye out for hostile Indians, they rebuilt rooms and installed an irrigation system. The Luceros and other citizens of Manzano, a tiny settlement nearby, began to build their village church near the old mission, only to be attacked in a series of Apache raids about 1830. The shell of the grand old mission church, La Purísima Concepción de Cuarac, which had lasted surprisingly well until then, was apparently torched in the fighting.

The story was similar at Abó. There was spotty subsistence farming and even a little sheep herding, but these were always isolated and dangerous settlements. The evidence in the village dumps indicates that Abó was periodically abandoned when Apache raids grew in number and ferocity.

When Mexico won independence from Spain in 1821, there was an official celebration up in Santa Fe, but the event went largely unnoticed in the remote farming area of the Salinas. The distant change in government did not make very much difference. Indian raids continued. Even when the Salinas became part of the United States in 1848, after the war between the United States and Mexico, the impact was hardly discernible.

Travelers who came through the old province took back reports of the three village ruins with their remarkable mission remains. About this time Las Humanas acquired a new name. The story of the "Quivira," for which Coronado had searched way back in 1540, was embellished in New Mexico folklore with wishful thinking about lost treasure. Quivira became Gran Quivira, the ephemeral prize for which everyone had been looking. No one knows who first attached the name to the cactus-covered ruins of Las Humanas, but it stuck. Thus in death the ruins acquired a name the village never had in life.

About 1900, in response to active advertising by the Territory of New Mexico, which was eager for immigration, the old Salinas Province began to be homesteaded. Many of the new immigrants came from Texas and Arkansas, which were experiencing hard times.

Ancient Indian fields and old mission farms became part of large dry-land farming operations, raising pinto beans. Everyone knew about the three great ruins, of course, and scattered smaller ones too. There were many childhood exploring expeditions among the falling stone walls, and vintage photographs show Sunday picnics by the missions.

The ruins of Las Humanas Pueblo, now called "Gran Quivira" by local people, were on federal land that had not been homesteaded. In 1909 President William Howard Taft proclaimed the ruins "Gran Quivira National Monument" under legislation that permitted him to set aside federal lands of particular scientific or historic importance. When the National Park Service was created in 1916, Gran Quivira National Monument came under its care.

In 1913 the Museum of New Mexico acquired the Quarai ruins from private ownership, but did not obtain clear title until 1932. In 1937 the ruins of Abó also came under the stewardship of the Museum of New Mexico, through purchase and donation by a group of University of New Mexico alumni. Thus all three ruins came into public ownership, and were made accessible to researchers and the general public. This split administration was simplified in 1980, when all three were combined into Salinas National Monument, a unit of the National Park Service. The name was later changed to Salinas Pueblo Missions National Monument.

Salinas Province is quiet now. Rural highways pass near the ruins, and the little town of Mountainair, site of the park headquarters, lies between the three units of the park: gray Gran Quivira on a dry ledge of the Chupadero Mesa; lovely Quarai with its faithful spring and grove of cottonwoods; and Abó, where red sandstone walls still tower thirty-eight feet high. Ragged stones that once echoed the Tompiro and Tiwa languages, then graceful Spanish, and finally English, now resound with the chatter of children spilling out of a school bus. For the park rangers, it's time to tell this remarkable human story again.

*(right) Four o'clocks and one-seed junipers.*

ISBN: 978-0-911408-98-0

Published by Western National Parks Association. The net proceeds from Western National Parks Association publications support educational and research programs in the national parks.

Receive a free Western National Parks Association catalogue, featuring hundreds of publications. Email: info@wnpa.org or visit www.wnpa.org.

Written by Dan Murphy
Edited by Ron Foreman and Randolph Jorgen
Design by Lawrence Ormsby and Carole Thickstun
Photography by: front cover: George Huey; inside front cover: George Huey; page 4: Russ Finley; page 14: Russ Finley; pares 23 and 25: Carol Chilton; pages 33–38: George Huey; page 39: Russ Finley; page 40: Russ Finley; page 59: George Huey; inside back cover: George Huey. All other photography: Lawrence Ormsby
Illustrations by Lawrence Ormsby
Printing by C&C Offset
Printed in China

Thanks to Joan Lloyd and Stephen Keane of the Western Archeological and Conservation Center, Tucson, Arizona, for help in photographing artifacts on pages 1, 5, 9, 13, 14, 17, 18, 19, 20, 21, 27, 45, 51, 55, 57, and 61.